WAKE UP! And live again, for a reason...

An Alternative to Suicide

Erik Batoog

ISBN-13: 978-1981943715

WARNING

Reader beware. The following words contain Truth. Perhaps you are not at the point in your life to accept all of it. Perhaps you will not be able to digest any of it. But perhaps you are. And if that is the case, you are at risk, my friend. You are at risk of losing the world that you know by opening doors to worlds that you have never known. And this may be dangerous for you. The following is not my biography. It does not contain the whole essence of me. But it does represent Truth that was deemed fit to be introduced to you right in the here and now. My hope is that you are one who needs this right now. If you do not believe that anything is wrong with your life, then perhaps you should stop reading right now. If, on the other hand, you are a brave soul ready to shout "Excelsior!", then sally forth my friend. And arm yourself with the wisdom that I struggled to produce for you. If you are afraid, then remember that you can always take everything with a grain of salt.

Books have a consciousness. I try to keep mine consistently good. However, you should understand that many factors could take you away from this. To investigate certain issues, you must necessarily delve into difficult spaces. If you feel like skipping my words, you can do that. Anyone CAN do that. It is selective. So you CAN try. This is very different than an author who forces you to read in a way that takes you into their worlds. If you do not want to see mine, that is your business. Know that you will not get a full understanding of everything. You may not see the Truth that you were looking for. Perhaps it was too much or perhaps you found a more convenient lie. If you are OK with that, you CAN read it that way. However, my intent is not to empower people to do bad things. These words were written so that YOU can be the best YOU. If you were the best you, then there would be no self-hurt or self-hatred. There would be good reasons to live again.

CONTENTS

ACKNOWLEDGMENTS

As always, I thank everyone who has had a positive impact on the development of my mind, body and character. This list primarily includes family, friends and teachers. But in recent years, it has expanded to include many random good people whom I have met (some of whom consider themselves servants of God, with and without any religious connotation) who happen to be willing and able to share some of their observations with me, a random stranger traveling in this place that we know of as the world.

1 A QUESTION

Ask yourself a question. This applies to anyone: young or old, white or black, barely alive or thriving. If you received an order, from your employer, your commander, your parent, your friend or whomever else and you knew that that order was wrong. Would you do it anyway? I believe that most people would say "No, I wouldn't do this thing. It's wrong." Perhaps some would say, "Well it depends on how bad it was. I mean I don't want to piss them off." And then a few may shrug and say, "Sure, why not?" What do you think you would do? And don't just say "It depends." Because we all know it does. Really think about it. Take your time.

If you said "No", then maybe these words will be good for you. Because most of this world is very hard on people who stand up for doing what's right over what happens to be beneficial to them. If you are finding yourself in times of trouble right now, then this could very well be the cause of it. Maybe you just broke up with your girlfriend because she wanted something from you that she didn't think you could provide. I'm sure that you tried your best, but you forgot something. Maybe your parents just got divorced and you blame yourself in some way. It wasn't your fault, but you forgot something. Maybe you just found out that your husband has been cheating on you and you don't know what to do. Perhaps something went wrong when you forgot something. Maybe your life is going perfectly fine, but you just have this nagging depression about you, that something isn't quite right. Well, you definitely forgot something. Everyone makes mistakes. And it's often because we do forget. But if you have the character to always do what's morally correct, then you can change the world.

2 SOMETHING TO REMEMBER

Always remember that there is hope. No matter who you are, what you have done, what you are influenced by at the moment, if you have life and are free to choose, then you can choose to do the correct thing. You can choose to do what is right in the moment, morally according to your own connection to the Universal Truth. You can get beyond the prisons that life has placed upon you and remember your true self, before that which bound you was properly known for the evil that it represented. Remember that while you are now free, you are still bound by the laws of the universe, which extend to all life. You must go beyond the habit of controlling or manipulating others for your own self-interest and enter the world of making decisions that are mutually beneficial to you and others. In the end, it is more about why you do something than what you do. That is why understanding is so important, because how can you really know somebody, whether or not that person is a friend to you, unless you know that person's motivation?

Love, as we know it in this human existence, is predicated on an ability to share something real with others. For some, this may mean that there is an understanding there, even if it is only a partial understanding. You can touch the underlying truth of somebody's soul without knowing much about their walls, but this will only matter for short-term relationships. For lasting, sustained, long-term relationships, you must get to know the whole of the person. What are they like in X situation? What are they like in Y situation? And this takes time. The first type of love is dangerous, because unless both people are honestly only looking for a brief bond, then this becomes an unequal situation where one person could get hurt. Now you can rely on your social group to assist you with your search, be it religious or otherwise. But never take such a thing lightly. For who knows if you might make a mistake and misconstrue a something at a sometime. Be honest with yourself so that you can connect with what is true internally and use it to guide you on your search. For if love is your guiding force, you can bring great joy to others. You can experience the truth of another. But if your love is being used for another's selfish wants, then it can also fail you and those you truly love. It can attract things that you do not want in your life. And that can hurt you just as much as it hurts other people. Where will you find your morality, your connection to your individual and social conscience at that point.

Understand the difference between sexual, emotional and spiritual attraction. Realize that you can be the sort of person who needs multiple people to satisfy these wants or can find it all in one. Or realize that you can satisfy all of these wants on your own and be happy with who you really are in a true, sustained way. This does not necessarily mean that you have to live a sheltered existence, blind to the evils of the world. But maybe it does. No matter what evils that you endured during your life, there must have been some serious good as well. You can draw on those things and recognize what is good about yourself to help see it in others. Perhaps you find yourself in a job that forces you to be involved in unsavory things. Well, then maybe it's time to think of a career change. Find ways to apply your skillset to something that you can truly feel good about supporting. If you are able to stop relying on others to support you, perhaps you can find people who are overjoyed to start helping you on your own path. So many people want to stand in front of the sun, deny you its warmth, and then demand that you share your resources for stepping away from it. Well, the sun is for all who are willing to let it in. The moon shines down on those who need it when their skies are clear. And the Earth is a home when you once again love what she is.

Miracles happen all around us, all of the time. It's just that some of us get stuck in a routine and others enamored with novelty. To see a true miracle, something that is undeniably a gift from a good place beyond your world, is a wonderful thing. That said, it has the potential of changing your mind forever.

We are all flawed, simply in our state of being human. Our spirit is restrained by our physical form. But that does not mean we can't be perfect in being the whole of who we are, mind, body and spirit. By accepting ourselves for who we really are, defined by our DNA and our experiences, we can fully experience life in the here and now. This will allow us to channel our time and energies to purposes worthy of us.

It can be easy to fall into a trap of negativity. Depression may very well be the natural male state in many modern situations. But that does not mean that one cannot control the influences within one that direct this sort of thinking towards suboptimal decision-making. Overcoming spiritual slavery allows one to divert that amazing energy to one's physical and mental processes. Through connection with influences that have one's best interest in mind, one can be the best person one can be. Connection to influences that do not have one's best interest in mind, on the other hand, threatens to distort one's outlook to subdue willpower and drain spiritual energy.

It is important to know your true self and there are many ways of trying to do this. I would recommend self-exploration first, disconnected from others. This way, one can get a less-biased look at oneself. Perhaps you can go for a solo hike in the wilderness, interact with Nature and see what she has to tell you about yourself and the world around you. Perhaps you can isolate yourself in your room and do research on the Internet. There is a lot of readily available information there. So perhaps technology can help you connect with your true self. Reading is a good outlet. Choose books about topics that are pertinent to the issues in your life right now. Try jump-starting your imagination. For it probably has developed a lot of rust over the years. Open up a book to a random page and point to a section of text. Apply what you read there to whatever issues are in your mind right now. For some, interaction with people is important. But always remember the Golden Rule. "Do unto others as you would have done unto you." A better way of thinking about it is "Only interact with those whose interaction will lift both of you up, instead of push one of you down." This is why one's influence over others is so important. If you have it, especially if you desire it, you must take special care that this influence is a positive one for both of you. Personally, I think it's best when you can be the only person in a room and be the life of the party. You could be in a room with hundreds of people and not talk to anyone. But if you can be happy in such a situation, then that is ultimately more important than what others may think of you. But everyone has different motivations in life. And it is through some of these that our influences drive us towards living in the ways in which we live. If you can identify what truly motivates you, then you can reveal a lot about your true self and path. Perhaps you will find that you do not like some of the things that motivate you. You may not want to be ruled by such urges. Well, you can work on those things. You can try to adjust your wants so that they are more in line with your needs as a person. For so often we confuse what we want with what we need.

Every family has its own habits and relationships between members. Every town and region has its own community norms. Every government has its own laws. Every religion has its own commandments. So, the extent to which you agree with all of those social groups ends up determining much of your practical character and affects how you make decisions. But churches and governments can be run by corrupt leaders and adopt systems that run counter to one's morality. Laws that were morally sound at one point in time may no longer apply today. So, how do you balance all of these varied influences and arrive at a correct moral decision? Well, it's important to be able to consult others. Ideally, one can think of a correct moral decision as one that maximizes the social good to all life. This is a complex decision and perhaps impossible for any one person. Much like counting calories in and out, this would take an unrealistic amount of tracking. So consultation becomes very important, especially when one's action impacts others. In general, here are a few guidelines for an exercise:

1) Determine your identity
2) Know the things that you simply cannot abide
3) Know that which you most admire in others
4) Be able to distinguish your needs from your wants
5) Focus on the long-term good of the many
6) Use these to form the basis of your code
7) Be open-minded, as most moral rules are relative

These steps will be useful to get your brain thinking about what really drives you and how you can start figuring out what's truly important to you. You do not have to be Moses seeing the Burning Bush, although it could help speaking to God. When it comes to interactions with others, focus again on ways to help lift everyone as opposed to ways that keep some pushed down. Blissful ignorance may make some people's decisions easy, but more knowledge of the effect of one's actions on others allows one to make more correct moral distinctions. Here are some things to think about. Have no fear, jealousy or other discriminatory bias. Do not base your code on these things. People develop protective barriers based on fear, but these fears are often based on misconceptions and can lead to wrong decisions.

3 ESCAPING PRISONS

For some, the world can be thought of as a giant cage with cages inside cages inside. If you find yourself in a situation that traps you, that gives you different options to do bad things, what choice do you have but to escape? You have to find a way to remove yourself from the situation. That could be having to change jobs. That could be a place. That could be people around you. That could even be simply changing your perspective on the situation itself. Somehow, you must imagine the problem and imagine further into a solution for that problem. And so often we don't know what the problem actually is. We might assign it to a specific thing or person, but the actual cause of that issue could be something or someone completely different. So, sometimes it's just easier to visualize the problem as something tangible in your mind. And pull the solution to that impediment from your creative self. Allow your creative self to give you the answer that you need to deal with the real issue.

For example, whistleblowers and prophets run into a lot of roadblocks that try to prevent them from communicating the truth to others. Companies and religious leaders try their best to shut them up, if not kill them entirely. They'll send their best assassins, their best attack dogs and their best manipulators to try to destroy the person's credibility to others or even their personal selves from the inside. And if you ever realize that this is going on, you may free your mind from it, but everything that locked you into that system before will still be present. So you have to stay on your toes to try to deal with the attacks that will come your way. As you adjust, they will adjust too. If you think that you know some of the evil in the world, chances are that you don't know a fraction of it.

What most everyone will choose to do is to give up. They will stop trying to fix the problems that they see and accept things as the world is showing them in the moment. But chances are that the world that you see right now is not the world as it really is. And what you feel are your most pressing concerns are not nearly as important as some things that you aren't even aware of. So, if you are a fan of the truth and actually fixing the problems in your life, then you can attempt to see things as they actually are.

Systems are like people. They will use you for their own purposes. They will stand in front of the sun and then charge you for getting out of the way. They will starve you and then try to feed you junk expecting that you'll be grateful. You can either submit and sell your soul or you can look deep within yourself for the answers that you need to find a better way. No religion has a monopoly on God. How can any one religion claim to have a perfect concept of what is unknowable unless one becomes omniscient? How can any government believe that its citizens are slaves, when the purpose of governments is to organize and help the people live? Mankind experiments with itself all of the time. It creates all sorts of systems to control and guide people along different routes. Well, do you want to listen to some human system, or do you want to listen to God/The Universe/The Earth? Often people confuse God with whatever social group happens to be controlling them at the time. God is above all of those instruments. God can speak to us in an infinite number of methods. But the demiurge can mimic God's voice and try to insert its own messages into you. So, you can either choose to listen to one of them or go the difficult route of creating your own connection with what Is. The Truth is the Truth is the Truth. What better God to worship than Him? Logic can be your Commandments, for every moral code has a logic to it. Do you have a personal "god"? Is that God to you, or do you distinguish between the two? Appreciation of your own interaction with God can help you distance yourself from thinking like a prisoner, even if you are in prison.

4 THE DOWNTRODDEN

Forgotten by society, poor wretched souls wander homeless, plagued by all manner of demons. They are persecuted by many they get near, as the world seeks to once again imprison them. Death would be a release for some, but the world doesn't allow it. So what can they do but drink and try to forget about all of the horrors that society has and continues to wreck upon them. The homeless, without mothers or fathers, get eaten up by a system that neither cares for their welfare or cares for their survival. They either get abused by surrogate families or have to turn to evil thoughts to protect themselves. Some get adopted into cults that teach them that their bodies aren't their own. They belong to the collective and can be used however the leaders see fit. Some get so brainwashed that they go their whole lives believing it. But these aren't even the worst off.

There are some unlucky souls who end up seeing traumas that should not even be thought of. They shrink from not only their conscience, but their very own soul. Such a process takes life right out of them, and they become the walking dead. They feel no pain. They feel no remorse. In fact, they feel no empathy for anyone but each other. They have lost all concern for humanity. So they treat them like dogs. No, they treat them like automatons, undeserving of any thought save in what ways that they can be of use. Having lost connection with their souls, they become incapable of feeling real emotion. So they subsist off the emotions of others, like parasites slowly draining the life out their hosts. Of course, this sort of state isn't exclusive to the dispossessed. Some of those who you believe to be the most influential people in society are the most possessed in this manner.

If you find yourself to be one of these poor souls, or even if you can empathize with some of their plight to some extent, then remember that you do not need to feed off others if you can re-find your inner conscience and become consistent with it. There is more than enough within you to feed yourself. But if you do not find that this is enough, then continue to ingest media from good sources. Continue to try to find people who will have your best interests in mind as opposed to those who simply want to use you for their purposes. I am sure that you have met enough of those types of people.

5 SELF-DETERMINATION

How is anything, the church, the government, the schools, absolutely anything external supposed to save you from anything in your past? They can empower you to do it. They can give you mentors to look up to and to model your life after. But any good one will simply help you promote the best of you. You should be making the change or risk becoming something else. At the end of the day, if you can't fix your own problems, others will be able to exploit your weaknesses. Sure, you can get together with friends. You can find causes to join that drive your attention to different points. But your underlying behavior within those groups will still be vulnerable to episodes from your past and, thus, to those enemies who would be willing to exploit and sell you to the highest bidder. This is the origin of control and the slave state that you know as life.

No matter who you think your parents are in your life, you can always see as a child of other parents. There will always be older memories than the ones your current life is based on, even if that means drawing from the beyond. Look to the past to fix the problems of today and the issues of today to fix the problems of the future. Your imagination, forged in the fires of the dreams of your childhood, will always be able to overcome the imprints that life has laid on you. It is simply the understanding of the self, within the context of the reality that you are living, that will allow you to free your mind.

While we are all bound to things in our lives, we are also all free to some level. True slavery is living death: not having a single thought or personal decision available to you. There are just varying degrees of freedom. Those that are at the top and those that are at the bottom often think of themselves as above the law. And they may be for most practical purposes. But all worlds have their own rules in a way. So there will always be a higher power, a higher judge.

Now if you do recognize that helping others helps yourself, then one thing that you could do is to focus on these people, the ones who really have not had the chances that you and I have had. The people who our societies and systems have treated the worst are the ones who all of us have the most responsibility for. This does not necessarily mean that you should pay every beggar who asks you for money. That may be a wrong thing to do for him or her in the long run. But yes, give food to the homeless who need it. Give them real help that will make a difference in their lives, even if it's just a smile or a hug. For I am sure that many would really appreciate such an act more than a dollar. When you remember that we are all connected, you remember that, on a higher level, we are all equal. So try not to be so quick to exclude somebody from a few moments of your life simply because of how they look or smell. You do not want to allow people to take advantage of you, but don't let the fear of that prevent you from making a positive difference in somebody's life. And remember the old aphorism, "Give a man a fish, feed him for a day. Teach a man to fish, feed him for a lifetime." To make a lasting positive difference for another is to remind both of you of yourselves.

6 MISCELLANY

To some people, the real world is yelling at people all day and polluting the environment with societal filth. They say that, in order to survive, you need all that negative energy and that blocking it out won't help. Perhaps this is the life of a fighter who eats negativity and focuses it in bits. Or is the truth that these vermin simply want to release the negative karma that they've accrued through their own actions and want you to take the hit for them? They want to avoid having to pay for the evil that they themselves did by transferring their guilt onto somebody else – just as they enjoy raping the minds and bodies of innocents around the world and use that trauma to control, they try to do the same thing to your souls. But such a thing is only a lie, as one's true soul can never lose the innocence and sanctity of life, no matter how much garbage is thrown on top of it. Furthermore, their selfish desire to pollute others isn't a real solution as well, as it simply deepens their debt with negative influences.

I normally do not agree on the sides. There's evil in all institutions, religions and governments for the course of what we know as the history of civilization. Thankfully, there's also been good. And these things can change. What is good in one year can serve evil in the future. But I like to think that the inverse is true as well. Who could keep up with such a rationalization? Admittedly, very few could. But that doesn't mean that some people shouldn't try. For example, the idea of feeding thoughts into somebody's head to give them insights enough to better himself and others may have started as a good one. But at some point, such a thing must have got hijacked by selfish people, using it to further their own ends and not those of the Community of Life.

7 FIGHTING WITH "THE DEVIL"

That which represents the leadership of all that is evil can be simple. And yet, to many, it is not something that can easily be defined in basic concepts. To say that the Nazis were pure evil, for example, could be true for some and yet still not completely true. Let's say you believe fully in "survival of the fittest." For what if we are about to get invaded by an alien species and fascist leadership is necessary to defend us? That could be used as a justification. One can counter that argument by saying, well survival isn't everything anyway. "Give me freedom or give me death." The true beliefs of the founding fathers recognized this. Perhaps they even saw a bigger picture in that our lives, such as we know them, go beyond the point of our birth and death. If this is the case, then how we live and what we contribute will end up being far more important than our constant survival. But then, survival is important and should be understood, if for no other reason than learning more about the world that we live in. So, you see how these arguments are circular and can be manipulated. People can take bits of them and say, "This is it. This is the answer." Well, that isn't necessarily correct. There are plenty of answers out there. But the important ones are the ones that you need for your life in the moment. The Truth can set all people free. However, it's just that most are not ready for it. Most cannot handle larger and larger amounts of the Truth. So we stay in our sheltered prisons. But do not delude yourself. For even if you know more, you will simply belong in a different prison.

Now you may be confused by now, or perhaps a little disheartened. Well, do not be. For our world sets up systems in such a way for these things to be clear for everyone. What side should you be on during a disagreement or conflict? Should you be on any side? That depends on what you believe in. Do you believe in sacrificing your life for your country or your family? Or do you simply believe in staying alive, or profiteering on the horrors inflicted on the victims of war? And then, all of that itself depends on the conflict itself. Imagine that it is a war. Is it truly a battle for existence, as some thought WWII to be, or is it simply a product of our own corrupted wants infringing on the needs of others? So, what you believe in and what you hold dear is what you need to remember. For that is your identity and will allow you to determine was is truly "good" to do in any situation.

This may seem like a difficult thing to do. It can be. For you may be surrounded by people who do not have your best interests in mind. You may feel threatened by the wants of others. And your needs may be the victim. I have been there and I know how that feels. It may seem like there is no hope at all. You have to choose between two things that you do not want to do. Instead of picking the lesser of two evils, always remember that there is another option. No matter what you are thinking right now, you can re-imagine your situation and break out of the prison that currently binds you to that thinking. So, your own path may be on the logical side. It may be on the creative side. If you are able to use both to their full potential, then what could stop you?

Peace, love, goodwill to man – these are all great things, concepts from a much better place than here. We should remember wisdom that such thinking originates. But in the application of such ideas to the world that we know, we must realize that, in a way, we are always at war. We are always soldiers in the battle of good vs. evil. We can choose to ignore this. We can choose to rise above much of this. But if our eyes are open to the Truth, then we cannot pretend that this doesn't exist.

Now, one may say, well, "What was once good is now evil" or vice versa. That would be incorrect. For it is not in the act itself that morality should derive. It more in the intention and the effects of such an action. So, if you want to accept more of the Truth, then do not worry as much about what you do per se and, rather, why you are doing it. Why are you supporting your political party? Do you always believe that they have the best answers for your country? No, the best president for a country depends on the time and place. It could be from one or it could be from the other. That doesn't mean that there isn't utility to identify oneself with a certain group. That's fine, but don't fool yourself into believing that you, or anyone else, is perpetually secure in that concept. And then, how do you define what's best for your country? Well, tie it into what's best for the entire planet and then you're getting somewhere. For there are many types of games. Some people think that they're all zero-sum. Well, they aren't. You can choose to play cooperative games where everyone wins simply by playing.

Now you may think that this is a lot to handle. You may think that in order for you to establish a practical moral code for yourself is too much of a burden. Well, on some level, it is. The more that you know, the less practical options you may have. By having to go through such intense mental calculations for every decision, you may feel restrained from doing any action at all. And yet this does not have to be the case. If you can find yourself and find your code, then you can establish it in your subconscious mind and allow that to guide you to make your decisions. All you have to do from that point is remember who you are if you ever lose your way. So what could seem to be a burden, what could seem to be restraining, can actually be freeing.

I don't know about you, but I'm sick and tired of the Devil (call it evil, call it what you will) having its way with the world and its people. Perhaps it is of our creation, a by-product of millenia of polluting the world with our disregard for life. Perhaps it is of another place and simply wants to go Home. Either way, we need to fix it within ourselves. We need to evolve into a higher state that can clean up the accumulated negativity of generations of humanity living in the dark. We need to find our freedom from its yoke and teach it that its only way back will be with a strong populace. Many people are too used to allowing the Devil to control them. The Devil can be thought of in many ways, but at heart it desires the destruction of your world. Were you ever made unhappy about your life, your friends or your family by an outside source? The source of that could have been controlled by or an actual agent of the Devil.

8 PRACTICAL FIGHTING

Sometimes the world may make it difficult to do work. Pretty much anything that you want to do, it could seem that it wants to do its best to prevent you. For example, let's say you write, it may make it as noisy an environment as possible and surround you with people: even if you go to a secluded spot. It could try to invade your thoughts in other ways, to make you confused or angry so that you're off-balance and can't think well enough to write. It's important to remember that this is, in most cases, not a specific person's fault. Perhaps it can be, but more likely people are being influenced by something else.

People want. All around the world. If you have something that they want, they will want to get at you. They will justify their actions to themselves in a variety of different ways, but it comes down to the same thing; they want to use you. The more valuable that you get to others, the more that they will want to use you. If you recognize this, what can you do about it? You may naturally want to close yourself off from others, so that nobody can take advantage of you. But this prevents you from interacting with good people whose company would lift the both of you. And it also distracts you from achieving the best sort of life that you could have.

So, continue to live, just be able to deflect the slings and arrows that are shot at you. Recognition of your worth in their eyes may be a part of that deflection process. For example, if you're a beautiful young woman, you can be assured that a variety of men out there will want to possess your body for something: sex, status, etc. Know this without letting it go to your head. That will allow you to recognize when a man is thinking in this way so that you can better interact with him. Hold out hope for interactions with men who don't have selfish drives motivating them to interact with you. (This could be one of the main reasons why women often enjoy socializing with other women and homosexuals, as the selfish sex drive issue is less prevalent).

There's a lot of evil in the world. Where does one start combating it? Right in front of you. Start with yourself and then extend it to the evil that you see around you. There's a lot of people around who try to take advantage of others. It's institutionalized. They learn to do evil from those that they learn it from. Socially, we're talking about issues like the effeminization of men and masculinization of women. To take a natural man and try to turn him into something more 'palatable' to society. This process of change removes him from his natural state, thus emasculating him. Men try to find ways to sublimate their natural selves in society, but these are, in the end, facsimiles of his natural state. Society's sensible attempts to better itself endanger the male's existence and threaten to trend the birth rate to 0 over the long term. In the modern world, homosexuality isn't necessarily a bad thing. Perhaps there are situations when men who cannot control their sexual appetites need to engage with other men. But these relationships must be consensual. Otherwise, they violate our common sense rule for human interactions. Manly friendship is going the way of the dodo bird, as society continues to teach males to impose their will over others. All men do what they must do in situations of scarcity. But with the realization of a world of abundance, why would a man feel the need to impose himself on others?

People seek to band together in groups for protection, strength in numbers and such. But if you have the ability to affect the world, then you need to make sure it's being used for good and not evil. So, do everything listed and look forward to death, as that will reunite you with your real family, in the end. Responsibility is what prevents you from being Nihilistic or death-seeking – responsibility to yourself, your family, your country, your species and Life in general. Avoid liars like the plague, as their lies originate in fear. What fear would a man of God possibly have of death? Thus, men of God have no real need to lie. Acceptance of their limited knowledge tends to make them talk less in unfamiliar situations, as one should be careful not to spread a misconception. Just such, true bravery lies in not attacking others out of fear, directly or passive-aggressively. So, understand those who do so for what they are: cowards, at the end of the day. They are afraid of losing something, of being hurt, of a variety of things. They are afraid of losing their jobs. They are afraid of losing social status. They are afraid of a variety of things and these compel them to do the wrong thing to others.

When people do evil to you, it is confusing to both you, the world in general and to God. Made in His image, the human race certainly didn't go as expected. Every generation brings new, confusing problems to figure out. Most people don't care to even think about the problems that face them, let alone those that they present others. So, what can you do to help show them that what they do is wrong? Be yourself. If you are true to yourself and God, then they won't be able to deny the Truth. Killing may have had a time and a place. But in this "civilized" world, where basic human needs are taken care of, how do you prevent young, undeveloped people from doing evil things? Well, we still have a traditional family structure. And yet, so many parents fail their children.

Perhaps we could require classes to be taken for any prospective parents. These classes could communicate concepts designed to achieve tangible goals: preventing bullying in the playground, fostering relationship-building skills, teaching respect for others and the importance to not abuse others, giving models for different examples of parenting skills, showing the importance of respecting your children as independent souls instead of your 'property', showing that spending time to find a way to make children feel what's important will be a better way of getting them to understand (no matter how much you want an easy solution), teaching them that anything that they do to another person should be agreed to by that person before it's done, the importance to not be too forceful with who you are as that can negatively impact other people, the importance of making one's own decisions in life (since connection with one's own soul will give one the ability to distinguish between doing what's right and doing what's wrong), the ability to distinguish fact from fiction as criminals will try to use all sorts of methods to lie to you and try to convince you to do the wrong thing – normally through peer pressure, or simply by being an asshole in your presence – realize that by just being around people who think evil things (because of having learned it or having been abused themselves) one's mind can get negatively impacted.

At some point, somebody has to be man enough and say 'enough is enough' and stop the cycle of abuse. When a person's basic needs are taken care of, then they don't have to settle for being abused by whatever system they have decided to follow. Society will threaten people with everything from poverty to death to force people to do the wrong thing. Who can possibly stand against it except for one whose mind is at peace with death? There were many who were against Christ because He empowered those without power. He stood up against the powers that be. And yet many of those did not want to be responsible for His death, as they knew that being responsible for hurting what is good or innocent can only be bad.

For some reason, the human animal can't handle some truth. Most can only handle a small portion of it. So, some of their solutions involve ridding themselves of extraneous information. The problem with this strategy is that it blinds them to the problems that they cause to others. So, they can only rely on blind faith to hope somehow that they are doing the right thing in God's eyes. For example, when a congregation's priest is accused of some impropriety, there will be those who deny that possibility. This continues the status quo. New truths will necessarily mean that minds will change. For example, slavers in the South who had a culture of taking advantage of others, had created a society where blacks were 'not human' and somehow different than them. So they justified their actions, continued to keep the blacks uneducated and wouldn't listen to any evidence of blacks who could think for themselves. Thus, denial of the universal truth of equality of all life continues to doom man to living in different types of inequality.

Lack of respect for one's soul creates lack of respect for one's children, other men and other living beings. (Ask yourself this parents, how can you really love your children if you don't respect them as individual living beings?) (Ask yourself this abusers, how can you really respect your own soul if you refuse to believe in something greater than yourself, if you continue to abuse others who still share the same connection with you that you did a long time ago? - few people would understand that) So think of something practical – that all depends on the person. Nationality has caused a lot of justification for wrongdoing over the years. But don't let the cause of eliminating nationality be the justification for wrongdoing. Everyone is presented with decisions to do what is right or to do what is wrong, no matter what living conditions they're in. So, stop blindly doing what other people tell you all of the time. Ask yourself, is it right? How can hurting another person ever be a right thing to do? Humanity learns these things slowly. Evidence of this is the elimination of slavery, the elimination of the death penalty, the elimination of war (in the future). But what to do about the pollution that society has created over the years, that continues to drag people down and make them continue to behave as if they're still in those situations? Society creates a lot of different ways to deal with this, but for an individual who wants to stand against this Devil, sometimes the only thing one can do is to simply refuse it. To stand up to Satan and tell him 'No' is a very, very difficult thing to accomplish, as the Devil will try to convince you in several different ways that the wrong thing is the right thing to do. And the Devil can take many forms. He could be inside of a friend or a lover, if only momentarily. Only you can see him, if you find the truth within yourself. Exposed thusly, you can refuse him.

One major problem with fighting the Devil is simply identifying him. Some will say that he doesn't exist. This is not true. Some will say that he is us. This is not true. He may be a product of us. Or he may be an external force. This fundamentally does not matter. Because he is there, real and has control over a great many people. So, a good man – more specifically, a man of God, can walk through life and be protected by good forces. But he will still face temptation. He will still face choices that threaten to take control over his physical and mental selves to constrict his spiritual. He must remember his connection with his soul, his connection with God. He must not be fooled by those forces that would mimic this connection. And he must always try to do the right thing, even when he is confused as to what that is. Liberation of one's energies can take many paths and these can lead to many different moralities.

One must remember that, even if "what is right" depends on context, it still is. There is always a right thing you can do and a wrong thing. It is not based purely on a facade. It is based on the existence of a Community of Life that binds this world. None of us individually may know the whole of this truth, but we know bits and pieces. And we can use this knowledge to help one another. We can help our shared vision of "what is right" directly and individually. To always be honest may be necessary, but so is admitting that one can never really "tell the truth" in the manner that one would want, at least with the forms of communication that we have access to right now. For telling somebody a truth does not necessarily result in that person coming closer to his or her own ultimate Truth. To do this, it may sometimes be necessary to speak indirectly and help another lead themselves towards their Truth. These two paths may represent fundamentally different methodologies. But as long as their goal is the same, they can be on the same side. Science and religion. Communism and capitalism. These things may seem at odds, but on another level, they are not. If they are used to guide us towards the Truth and a better relationship with the Community of Life, then they can coexist peacefully. The Devil, plain and simple, does not care about us. The Devil will use us to get what he wants, whether that's getting him somewhere or destroying the Community of Life. He does not care about you or I. He fundamentally does not care about any human. To him, we are like robots without any life force. It is up to you to remind him that you do have a soul, no matter what he's done to it in the past. And you can use the power of that soul responsibly. You can use all of your influence in this world for the good of all, for God and for Truth. If you already have great power but it is coming from him, then you may know that he is working his evil through you. You should stop feeding him, even if it means rejecting all of that power. The Devil uses many lies to try to convince you to do evil to others. He will say that they're the enemy. He will try to convince you that an entire group of people are bad, just because of some difference. He will say that others are evil so you must hurt them or even kill them. He will try to imprison your mind and body in many ways. He will say it's justified. Don't let him. Have faith that, if the time ever comes, you will be guided to do what you must do. The Devil's minions like the Earth way too much, since it is much better than the alternative. Let's take it back from them. Let's remind them of what the true power is. Let's remind them of the Truth.

Sometimes it may seem like it's you against the world. When the Devil has control, it can seem like this to men of God. He will surround you with his agents so that everyone you turn to may not be forthcoming with you.

This is not a happy situation. But you can and will withstand it. You will not blame them for the evil that they do. For they cannot control themselves. They are being influenced by the Devil. Instead, you will be able to find new people to form relationships with, new friends. Once you are on the path, follow it. Use your good thoughts and the tools of this world to connect with good people. There are many different groups of people on Earth, many different ways to interpret the Truth of God. He will show you the path to the ones that will resonate best with you. They may be religious. They may not. If they are, celebrate your shared belief in God, even if yours differs. If they are not, do not beat your ideas over their heads. A portion of the human race holds negative feelings towards any concept of God because humanity has used such to justify doing the Devil's work at times in the history of the church. Understanding of this allows you to coexist with anyone, religious or atheist, as long as they are on the correct path. Those people will not try to manipulate you. Or maybe they will and just not be able to succeed, who knows? I would like to think that they wouldn't seek to manipulate you into changing, or try to beat you into submission. You may think otherwise. You may believe that the only way to change somebody is to force them to change. This is not true of men of God. For once they are on the path, only they change themselves. Manipulation and force only serve to anger them, and, thus, to anger God. This is not something that anyone should want to do.

Perhaps it would be useful to remind you of the sheer arrogance of humanity to wholly believe in any single concept of the Truth or of God. For none of us is individually or socially omniscient. We can connect with God. We can experience perfection and Heaven. Prophets do this. But I wonder if those experiences exist outside of time and space. And what they bring back to this world, can it really ever represent the Truth completely? It may allow them to help the world. It may give them insights that have never been thought of. But to close your mind off from all other contact with the Truth simply to support one concept over another, wouldn't that be a shame? People die for far sillier things in this world. But I would hope that one day, men who follow the correct path could choose life, love and God's Truth. For anyone who truly knows God will know that our attempts at conceptualizing him have been, to this point, imperfect. We have had, and continue to have, timely inventions in science and religion that stem from His influence. But often when we try to consecrate these works, we end up handing them over to the Devil. And that is a great shame. For the powers and inventions derived from good should not be used for evil.

9 LINCOLN

"That which is not just is not law." The Universal laws override any of man's laws. Because they are just, while the laws of men are often not. "Are we free? Or are we slaves under mob law?" Who can say that they're truly free? We're always imprisoned in some way. And the more that we free our minds, the more difficulty we often encounter from those who would want to enslave us. "As a nation, we began by declaring that 'all men are created equal.' We now practically read it 'all men are created equal, except negroes' When the Know-Nothings get control, it will read 'all men are created equal, except negroes, and foreigners, and Catholics.' When it comes to this I should prefer emigrating to some country where they make no pretence of loving liberty -- to Russia, for instance, where despotism can be taken pure, and without the base alloy of hypocrisy."

I wonder what Lincoln would be thinking now, seeing what his beloved country has become. Here is a man of principle, a politician who went against the grain and stood for what he knew to be right as opposed to what he believed would help his career. He stood and fought for freedom over oppression. As a lawyer, he fought for justice. What would happen to him in today's America? People would laugh and deride him. People would call him "a relic" or "awkward." In fact, he may have had to deal with that in his day, but he still fought. "Those who deny freedom to others deserve it not for themselves, and under a just God, cannot long retain it" How can anyone who knows a bit of the truth believe that what rules your government today is just? Every country has its problems, but Freedom and Justice? The powers that be spit on these things daily. They use them as tools to delude everyone else. They enslave you with the very ideals that you hold dear. They try to convince you that everyone else is doing the things that they are doing themselves, compelling you to blame the wrong things. The problems are many. Many of them revolve around the same concepts that have been driving the world since the dawn of civilization. Those in power want to stay in power. They try to pass on their power to their children, whether they were good parents themselves, whether or not their children are suited to power. So inequality continues to grow and our home becomes increasingly more like the despotic influence that we escaped in the first place. In the United States, it comes in the form "Taxation without Representation." The Founding Fathers did not stand for this, so why do Americans today?

10 RELATIONSHIPS WITH MEMBERS OF THE OPPOSITE SEX

It can be important to not give too much to a person too early. In general, you shouldn't engage sexually with her/him unless you see an opportunity for future growth there. It's important, in any relationship, that both of your understandings of exactly where the two of you are is in sync. In order to arrive at this, it's normally a good thing to select people based on criteria that will allow you to distinguish between those who may and may not be able to get on the same page as you.

Misogyny and misandry, both from the same source and both causing pollution to our social environments. This does not mean that men have to be more feminine and women more masculine. What's needed? Open and honest communication and expression of one's true self. With this, technology, the universe, God, or simply the magic created between two people will prevail. However you want to think about it, honesty and open communication are necessary for relationships to to truly blossom between equals, to go beyond simple expedience and into something useful spiritually. Faith in love is great. I still have faith in love, although not much in attraction. But the means by which some of our systems selects people to be together are obviously flawed. One can hold out hope for the sort of significant other that stories are written about, instead of for. But would it not be better to be happy with what you already have? I refuse to give up on either gender for I do believe that all of their relational problems stem from a misconception of the other. And then again, perhaps the solution is far more simple. Perhaps the most elegant solution is that which turns the "Battle of the Sexes" into the "Battle for the Sexes." Allow women to be women and men to be men.

Sewers are an important concept to groups of humanity who produce a lot of waste. The polluted spirits of several people in power in their communities have forced them to develop methods to siphon much of their waste onto others who are unaware of the negative impact of this behavior. The human manifestation of such systems can show themselves as simple harmful gossip all the way to sexual/spiritual abuse of children. These systems keep those in power in power and everyone else in the dark. For if any man of God realizes the depravity that is actually happening in much of the world, to whatever degree, he would most definitely question it and try to do something about it if possible. Such methods of abuse can assist societies in separating people into specific roles. For example, if a society really needs soldiers for a war, men will stand up and do what needs to be done, from a responsible place. Think WWII. However, the artificial creation and maintenance of unnecessary war machines necessarily create pollution into the world and, more importantly, into the society itself. The maintenance aspects, for example, are so abysmal that one wonders if it's worth it to maintain these sorts of machines at all. Kidnappings, brainwashings and all manner of abuse (that will definitely prevent one from entering Heaven) used by different groups are not only inefficient in a social welfare perspective, they are debilitating to a society. They are why Rome fell and will be why America will fall unless its people are able to change these things. Too many people associate groups led by corrupt actors or methods that dominate certain systems as the systems themselves. They think oh, I puff out my chest so that is what makes me a man. I wave my flag around and that is what makes me a patriot. I identify with X and turn a blind eye to the abuses done in the name of X. Well, nothing could be further from the truth at the end of the day. For the true patriot and the true man of God can know that what is truly good for his country is also what's good for everything else in his life, including his religion and his family. The fears that drive men directly or indirectly to hurt other people are exactly the things that keep them down and prevent them from understanding more of the Truth. It has nothing to do with one's sexuality. It has everything to do with one's spirituality. The same methods that serve to get those in power what they want sexually (be it straight out forced sex slavery or be it the emasculation of men) are what prevents their souls from getting what they need spiritually and what drives them as social groups to literal and figurative failure. This touches upon what is wrong with some of the systems in the world today.

11 WHAT THE WORLD NEEDS NOW

Consideration of what one wants to ultimately do in life has a great impact on a lot of other decisions. When you are still in school and thinking about what you want to do, or even if you have had a long career but aren't happy with it, you should consider how the world works now, the trends in job markets and what skills will be important in the future. I see a few important factors going on right now. This is the age of Globalization and Environmental Crisis. Countries are becoming more connected in a lot of ways and people are beginning to focus more, as they should have long ago, on environmental concerns. Also, we're getting more and more populated as a planet. And technology is improving at an exponential rate. This is leading to tremendous stresses on our resources and more competition for fewer jobs. So, the jobs of the future may be far different than the jobs of today. Perhaps you can be thinking of a new product or a new method of selling a product. Perhaps you can take up a job in something that is always in demand, like Healthcare for example. Or perhaps you don't even need a job at all. If your passion is in some obscure art or institution that has gone out of popularity, do it anyway. Be the last traditional tattoo artist. Be the last flame-eater. Even if you don't develop a large consumer base, your passion will propel you forward and you will more than survive. You will thrive. And by keeping that tradition alive, you will be doing a great service to us all. So often we miss out on important lessons in native cultures by ignoring them completely. We need a living history of ourselves as a people and such things matter, no matter how out-of-style they may be.

The American culture, and increasingly most of the world, is ingrained in a greedy form of capitalism. This system developed with Adam Smith and others who believed in the power of self-interest to motivate. And this has proven to be the most effective economic system (on a large scale) that the world has yet seen. But self-interest does not equal greed. And most people fail to realize this. Self-interest exists in an honest consideration of one's true utility function that includes the welfare of others (for most persons). By ignoring this, people focus on making money. It becomes its own creature. The rich start to use it as a means of keeping score in a sick-and-twisted game of power and control. This is ultimately damning for any system and our recent increase in income inequality demonstrates this.

So, do not allow money to be your focus. I grew up poor. I know that money matters. You need enough to be comfortable and to support your family. But it should not be your primary motivation if you care more about living a good life. Our media and arts culture promote beauty and fame. These things aren't necessarily bad, but do you want them to guide your life? Do you want to be guided by those who do? The less that you need them, the more beautiful and famous you will feel, no matter how many people compliment or recognize you on the street. Besides, beauty and fame can be negatives for many people. They can attract a lot of unwanted attention. This can make the possessors build up heavy walls to block all of it out. Sex is a great thing. It always has been. But do you want to spend all your time and energy pursuing sex? Well, maybe you believe that you do. And God bless you for it. But these days it is simple enough to pleasure oneself. And I am sure this will be more and more true in the future as we develop robotic companions.

Do not get me wrong. I am not saying that celibacy is the answer for everyone. It can be an answer for some, but often marriage is a sensible solution. And statistics have shown that arranged marriages without premarital sex often lead to more lasting relationships, controlling for cultural factors. If you're an American, sex has certainly become more prevalent since the Sixties/Seventies. People are doing it at earlier ages and putting off marriage until later ages. This may allow some people to come to better understandings of variety in relationships. Some may call this "finding themselves." But is it really? Or is it simply allowing ones wants to be modified by interactions with others over time while ones needs stay the same? I am not saying any of these things are necessarily morally bad or good. I'm saying that it's important to think about these issues and what they really mean to you. When you narrow down your foci to that which is really important, think about engaging in activities guided by those things as well as the concept of mutually beneficial interactions.

Today, there are a lot of people who feel like they've been "thrown to the wolves" by society. They feel like they're not wanted or they've been so abused by the people and systems around them that they no longer care for certain groups. If you are one of these, then hopefully you have a loving family or loving friends that you can fall back on. But if not, then always remember that you have yourself. And if you can remember how to start loving yourself, you will be able to break out of a lot of the problems that you are facing now and start being able to reintegrate yourself into a society that, although it may not realize it, does need you. Loving and respecting oneself means thinking and doing in ways that one respects. Some of our more fascist systems will try to convince people that certain traits and characteristics are more beneficial to it. Perhaps an influence in your life encouraged you to develop in a certain way that is not and was never your true purpose. These things can be overcome, but change like this can be difficult. And even if you are able to spend the time and effort to do this, there are some who feel so trapped that they cannot. There will always be somebody who has had it worse than you. There will always be someone whose life was more wrecked and thrown off-path. So approach people like that with sympathy, or even empathy. Because you may certainly be in a position to help them.

Movies, TV, concerts, books and all other sorts of media can have a large effect on us. If we ingest enough of them, they can even start to imprint themselves on our unconscious minds. So, it's important that we are careful to make sure we are limiting our consumption to things with messages that really resonate with ourselves. Sometimes we can be gathering the wrong messages from these things. Not all messages are from the places that we want to be listening to. So if you start to feel a compulsion to do something that your conscience knows is not the right thing to do, then this could demonstrate a problem. Because if you were internally consistent, then you shouldn't start getting the urge to do what you know is wrong in your own moral code. Now, perhaps you've adopted another's moral code. Perhaps you follow a certain religious leader who has listed certain things to be wrong, even though you're interested in them. Well, be honest with yourself. If you are still going to follow that leader, then you will have to change your own moral code to be a faithful follower. Or if you know that your own moral code is more correct, then why are you listening to that leader in the first place? Perhaps you feel that you don't follow any leader at all. Perhaps you feel that you are completely free and able to make your own decisions. Was that an honest assessment, or are there still people out there who influence your decisions more than your true self?

Also, much of mainstream America has lost turning its eye to Church and State. People have become so frustrated with the corruption and inefficiency of their churches and government that they give up on them altogether. Well, these things will have to change for the better if we want to survive. In the meantime, if you find yourself in doubt when you once were a believer, try to remember what first drew you to your church or government service. Try to remember what messages really resonated with you. And embrace those. Imprint those in your consciousness so that they can become incorporated into your unconscious. I find that often, the beginnings of lasting systems are some of the most insightful. If you are American, think of the United States. Think of the Declaration of Independence. "We hold these truths to be self-evident, that all men are created equal, that they are endowed by their Creator with certain unalienable Rights, that among these are Life, Liberty and the pursuit of Happiness." These are important words that have somehow been lost in the modern American identity. All are created equal, and yet we treat some as no better than animals. We abuse others with our words and actions from a false place of superiority. All of us have the right to life and yet we kill each other as if we didn't have that right. We have the right to be free, but all we seem to want to do sometimes is enslave each other. While all of us have some ability to pursue our happiness, many have little ability to put food into their family's stomachs. And this does not afford them the time to pursue other things that may make them happy. Now if you are from another country, think of the founding principles that founded your country. I'll bet that there are a lot of good concepts there that have been lost to corruption or even a simple inability to understand and translate into the modern world.

Some people may want to believe that it's easier to simply to give up on all governments, all religions and everything else that have ever hurt them. Or better yet, they want to think that they can form something else to replace these systems. Well, instead of Nihilism or destruction, why not try an honest attempt at improving them first? Perhaps you have tried to no avail. Well it may be time to take another approach. Start with yourself and then extend this outwards. Find your own true conscience again and this will allow you to express your opinion as a citizen or follower in all ways. You will be able to vote independent of bias. You will be able to participate in community functions with something valuable to give: yourself. And you will be valuable once you find yourself on your true path again.

12 GOOD AND EVIL

If you live, then only you can ultimately decide on what is the right thing to do anytime you make a decision. On the other hand, your identity and, thus, your moral code will be determined by all of the influences in your life, including the people. So, while on the one hand you need to figure out what is right for yourself, you also need to accept that everyone in your life is essentially a part of that process. Thus, many would find it easier simply to adopt a set of religious commandments to drive their decisions. This is fine, but one must still interpret them in the modern day. There are a lot of moral insights in religious texts that can be taken out of context. So if you want to adopt these moral stances with an eye towards the Truth, you must really try to conceive of their actual meanings to you. Perhaps you can read the whole book, get a feeling of what is being spoken about and then apply these ideas to your own life.

Let's take a look at some Old Testament commandments, as these apply to both Christianity and Islam as well.

1 – Thou shalt have no other gods before me. Since God is omniscient, He knows all. He is essentially the Truth. So what other gods could be higher than Him? Now you may be thinking of God in a different way, but that will essentially form the set of options that you have to whatever that concept is.

5 – Honor thy father and thy mother. If you have a family, it is important for you to do your personal best to do them honor. There are bonds of

blood that run deep and connect you. And if they never treated you well, you may feel like severing that bond. You should still do your best to honor them, even if you end up rarely seeing them in person.

6 – Thou shalt not kill. The power of life and death is not in your hands. Do you have a license to kill? It is one thing to defend oneself from an attack. But it is another thing entirely to actively seek out the death of another, whether you pull the trigger or order it to be done. All are complicit in murder, but the original intent matters most, as it would not exist without that. The will to violence can be a natural one, but there are always other options. One can always look for alternative solutions if they are not actively at war.

7 – Thou shalt not commit adultery. If you want to sleep with another, you owe it to your spouse to communicate that urge before acting on it. For that very communication may save your marriage. Betraying the trust you've developed over time will not.

8 – Thou shalt not steal. If something belongs to somebody else in all reasonable ways, then it is not for another to take it away. If it is a public good, then it needs to be properly cared for and shared.

10 – Thou shalt not covet. This demonstrates that jealousy is not a good thing. In fact, jealousies can develop weaknesses in one's mind that make one vulnerable to "the Devil."

These things should be taken for what they are: common sense. They can be blindly followed. But perhaps for you, it would be better to really get to understand them so that you can apply them to your life. Incorporate them into your own moral code, which is essentially common sense rules developed from one's true nature.

Knowing more and more Truth about the world reveals the true sources of your pain and hardship. Perhaps there are those who you love unconditionally. Well, they may be under the influence of other things. Or perhaps you are and you are infecting them with it. What has truly defined your concepts of right and wrong? Chances are, a lot of the stories of your childhood made a difference. Were these spoken to you? Did you read them? Did you watch them? Or did they just happen to find you, like dreams coming to the rescue? Whatever the method, you do know which ones are helpful and which ones can be let go into the night. Finding yourself is a lot like remembering yourself. Do you remember what made you truly happy, beyond all of the social conditioning? Because it still will, you just have to translate it into your new vocabulary. I know that the pain of life can be overwhelming at times. And sometimes you just want to give up. You want to start believing that there is no hope, that you are eternally damned to a particular life or a particular place in the world. Well, I am here to tell you that there is hope. There is always hope. You just have to remember what is important in life.

Perhaps people deflated the bubble of your ego a long time ago. Perhaps your ego is so huge that it overshadows all who come near you. Well, both are an illusion. For if you can remember who you really are, that you are a part of the Universe, a member of the eternal army of Truth, a Child of God, then you find the Truth within yourself. And this, my friend, is a source of more pride than any amount of ego could ever hold. You are a survivor. You have accepted the responsibility of your life to be who you were meant to be. And you will continue to do so until it is time to go Home. Do not be fooled by those who will try to convince you otherwise. Do not allow people to step in front of the Sun and charge you to step away from it. Be yourself and you will free yourself. And that will allow you to attract good people into your life. For there are good people who, like you, only want what's best for all. Yes, there are plenty of others who have chosen to be ruled by various evil influences, but you do not have to be one of them.

I have bounced these ideas off of others. I have refined them. I continue to be open to doing so. For if you visualize the Truth as a line, from ultimate falsehood to ultimate truth, one is constantly able to move further towards the Truth or further away. This is why if you are living a lie, then it is so easy for bits of Truth to move you towards it. This is why it is important for you, if you have achieved higher truths, to preserve them and protect them from the lies that you will face in life.

Perhaps you are a veteran returning home. You are used to a militaristic structure, where people have ranks and those with lower ranks follow orders. Perhaps you've awaken to some truths behind the facade of war, the real motivations behind the battles you fought. Perhaps you were simply infused with so much negative energy that your brain can't seem to find its way out anymore. Well, the Truth can set you free. Try to come to an understanding of what's really bothering you. What are those things nagging at you from before you joined the military? Why did you join in the first place? Where did those feelings and urges come from? If it was simple patriotism, great. You may feel less patriotic now. Well, you do not have to. For those that may have taken advantage of your patriotism are the ones in need of lessons in how to be a good citizen, not you. Those who tried to buy your soul with whichever sort of false dreams they were selling failed. For your soul is still alive. You just have to find it again. You just have to break it free from their hold over it. Now, this may not be what you want. You may want to stay in darkness and simply find a way to coexist in the civilian world. Well then, perhaps you want to continue lying to yourself and others. Perhaps you want to use those lies to protect yourself from those who would care for you and to protect those from the tremendous pain and strife inside of you. They tried to tell you what being a man really meant. They tried to convince you what being a patriot meant. Is that working for you? If not, then they were wrong. Before your country even existed, there were people around. They had a different understanding of being a responsible person, a good man or a good woman was. And this understanding was just as important. Perhaps it's time for you to remember a more natural state of being alive. Perhaps you can shed light on the lies that cloud your mind from yourself. Perhaps you just didn't like the people that you had to work with, but were convinced to start empathizing with them. Perhaps you need to find people who speak your real language and who may care about you. No matter what the case, much of the bad that happened was not your fault. During WWII, it was important for people to step up and take responsibility for everyone's defense. People rose to the challenge because it was the right thing to do. Today, the reasons for war and for society selecting certain people to go there are different. And if you can come to terms with the truth of it, then you can realize this, make amends and move on with your life.

13 PROTECTION

There are a lot of ways that people protect themselves from other influences. I recommend that you find your own. But here are some ideas.

Be patient. Patience is a virtue and there are good reasons behind that. Try to be patient with yourself. If you are not coming up with the feelings and/or ideas that you know you need, then there is something wrong, or something wrong happened in the past. So continue to work on it and don't punish yourself further by becoming frustrated with yourself. Be patient with others. For they don't know what you've been through or even the entirety of what you're going through. People have a tendency to see themselves in others. So when they see something that has troubled them in the past, they may recognize it in you, even if it's not really what's bugging you.

Clothe yourself in the armor of Truth. People may fear you. They may fear losing control of you. Or they fear the truth within you. They want to continue their lives in blissful ignorance of the evil that they do. They want to continue to delude themselves into believing that they are perfect people, no matter how much harm they do to the Community of Life. So they beat you down. They try to make you feel small and insignificant. But if you can find the Truth within yourself, then you will remember who you are. You will remember why you are here. And you can face any attacks or challenges that come your way by holding onto that memory.

Find that you are not alone in your struggles. There are good people out there who want to help you. Perhaps they are being prevented by others. Perhaps it is you and your inability to fully be yourself that is preventing them. Perhaps sometimes you feel like the entire world hates you. Well, it is only because of what you represent to them. In reality, those people hate themselves. Express yourself honestly with them and they'll get the picture. Either they will realize that you're a good person who should be treated well, or they will shrink away and stop bothering you as much.

Understand the concepts of social dynamics. The more honest with yourself you are, the more of an impact you will have on others, whether or not they even realize it. Since fear motivates many of them, they may consider you from a "different tribe" and try to wage war with you. Protect yourself, but never allow their limited understanding of your truth to affect it. Do not allow their fear and hate to convince you that you are something that you are not.

Obey the laws of Truth and then the laws of man. The laws of man are important. They maintain peace in a chaotic world. But they are not perfect. Our justice system can often be corrupted by the influence of money and politics which can be flawed. But the laws of Truth do not change. And they are far more important. Find them within yourself and adhere to them. They will be your guiding lights in times of trouble. They will help you make the correct decision when you're faced with a difficult one.

Survive. You are here for a reason. You do what you do for a reason. You are born and you die. Perhaps this is true for your human form, but you can believe that part of you continues on, whether this is in the DNA that your children possess, the memories of you that exist in the world somewhere and/or the very soul that dwells within you. Believe in that, as it will give you hope and a sense of responsibility to soldier on.

Align your wants with your needs. Over the course of our lives, we are convinced that we should want a lot of different things, through envy, jealousy or otherwise. Do not allow these things to disquiet you and make you make bad decisions. For what you really need is far more important than the wants that you've developed over time. If you can adjust what you want to make them more in line with your underlying needs, then you eliminate the ability of others to manipulate your wants to get you to work for them.

Know your enemy. They can come in many forms. They can be emotional vampires trying to drain you of your life. They can be master manipulators trying to force you to do what they want you to do. They can be sensations of hopelessness or defeat that make you want to give up on everything. They can be your own memories reminding you of when you weren't on your true path. Identify them and face them on whatever field of battle that you choose. If you don't want to fight, then learn to avoid them in a way that doesn't steer you from your path. Remember, there are many people who are playing some sort of game with each other. Allow them to play their games while you play the most important game of all: the battle for your true soul.

Find your true loving self and be able to express it honestly. This can mean different things for men and women. But it's not just about sex. It's about empathy and compassion. It's about loving yourself enough to allow yourself to be. It's about caring enough for another person to share the truth with them.

Develop your moral code. The world is getting ever more complicated, as systems stay in place and new ones are developed. You must know what's right for you to do in this world. You must know where to draw a line in the sand and say "No more! You shall not pass!" Feel free to share your viewpoints with those you trust, but be hesitant to allow them to infringe upon the viewpoints of others.

To survive in the midst of chaos, imagine yourself as a giant and every bit of it is simply a gnat or a miniature arrow, bouncing off your thick skin. Or imagine a battlefield, with death and destruction all around you, and you walking out into the middle of it, without fear, like Stonewall Jackson or Wyatt Earp. The bullets whizzing past you, unable to touch your invisible armor. And while all of this is happening, you look for the general of the enemy's army, ready to walk up to him, aim your gun and tell him to surrender.

14 ANOTHER WARNING

You may think that we will never meet so I have no interest in actually helping you. Well, I am writing this for you. Yes, I am writing this for me as well. I felt compelled to do this. Perhaps it was seeing the constant blight of people making the wrong decisions. Instead of looking to capitalize on those, I think to help. There may be others reading this book right now who think like the former. Well, maybe they deserve the fate that they're in. I know that there are those who do not. Regardless of whether or not we actually meet, I may have known a person like you, a phantom of the self that you find yourself to be. It is extremely unlikely that we had any sort of close relationship. However, I was around you enough to notice something. And it is a mistake that many of you make over and oer again. It is just like that last sentence. You miss the "v." What the "v" is in your life depends on you. Often your expectations and your perceptions, clouded by those of selfish mind, block you from accomplishing what you really wanted to do. Sometimes you lose sight of what you want. That may be fine, because as long as you knew, then you can be on the path. Some may believe that it is "too much" to go outside one's box and to honestly understand one's life within the context of a greater world. Well, that is not what I was wishing for. It was coming from a more personal place to you. Remember, your box got you to this place. Your box has failed you, just as it has succeeded for the rest of the box. So you can stay in your box, live the life that you know – maybe you will stave off some of the worst of it for a while. However, you will still be in that box. You will still have failed to fix those problems that cause your box to turn on you in the first place.

So what is the solution if that does not work for you? Start to love your box again. Start to be the person that your box wanted you to be in the first place. Start doing the things that your box wanted you to do. That has nothing to do with me. I am probably not a part of your box and you don't want to have anything to do with going outside of your box, do you? It is a choice. Choose your path. Go your route. If you believe that another source of information has been more useful for you, that is your choice. Did the creator care more for you? Maybe you slept with that guy. Maybe you knew that woman more personally. Well, did I write these words to get something from you? One reason that I wrote these words is because I wanted to write something as important as any of the great works that I read growing up. Somewhere along the way, I accomplished things even greater. So instead of writing the book to end all books, I wrote this one for you.

Yes, there are many parallels to my thoughts and others. And yet my thought is not dominated by any others. I succeeded in that. This is a testament to that journey. I do not even need to write these things down. By the nature of thought and how it interacts, this book will not convey everything that I would in its place for many who will read it. At least I tried. At least I did not stand on the sidelines while masses of people who could have been helped fall by the wayside. At least I did not stand idly by while selfish minds played with the lives of others for personal benefit. No, I am me. If those things that form your perception of the world allow these words to help you, great. If I have assisted you in understanding what you needed to understand in a higher and more complete way, great. If somebody else has taken many of my words and published them under another name, then they suck. However, I am not that person. I am not those people. And yet, by extension, perhaps that is not entirely true. These words come from my experience and the experiences of others as understood by me and have a life of their own.

ABOUT THE AUTHOR

Erik Batoog is a man who has been through a lot in life. But despite it all, he tries to keep a childlike mind, ready to creatively deal with current challenges and those on the horizon. He spent far more than enough years in school to write this book. Studying a variety of subjects including literature, theology, language, history, economics, psychology and philosophy, Erik enjoyed much of his time in academics. Some of his favorite pastimes have included throwing a piece of cork wrapped in cowhide as fast as possible past people holding sticks, making dents in large leather containers of sand, expressing himself artistically, enjoying others expressing themselves artistically and searching for a Grail ready to be filled with clean water.